LEVEL 3

Sonia Sotomayor

Barbara Kramer

NATIONAL GEOGRAPHIC

Washington, D.C.

**For Callie and Kinsey, who are
on their way to becoming strong women
like Sonia Sotomayor —B. K.**

Editor: Shelby Alinsky
Art Director: Callie Broaddus
Editorial: Snapdragon Books
Designer: YAY! Design
Photo Editor: Christina Ascani
Special Projects Assistant: Kathryn Williams
Rights Clearance Specialists: Michael Cassady & Mari Robinson
Design Production Assistant: Sanjida Rashid
Managing Editor: Grace Hill
Production Editor: Michael O'Connor
Manufacturing Manager: Rachel Faulise

Library of Congress Cataloging-in-Publication Data

Kramer, Barbara, author.
  National geographic kids readers : Sonia Sotomayor / By Barbara Kramer.
     pages cm
  Includes index.
  ISBN 978-1-4263-2289-1 (pbk. : alk. paper) -- ISBN 978-1-4263-2290-7 (library binding : alk. paper)
  1. Sotomayor, Sonia, 1954---Juvenile literature. 2. Judges--United States--Biography--Juvenile literature. 3. United States. Supreme Court --Biography--Juvenile literature. I. Title.
  KF8745.S67K73 2016
  347.73'2634--dc23
  [B]
                                              2015027917

The publisher and author gratefully acknowledge the expert content review of this book by Joan Biskupic, author of *Breaking In: The Rise of Sonia Sotomayor and the Politics of Justice* (2014), and the literacy review of this book by Mariam Jean Dreher, professor of reading education, University of Maryland, College Park.

**National Geographic supports K–12 educators with ELA Common Core Resources.
Visit natgeoed.org/commoncore for more information.**

Table of Contents

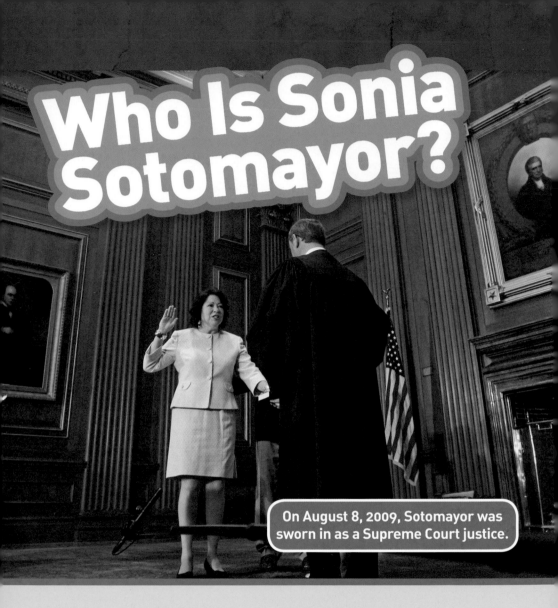

Who Is Sonia Sotomayor?

On August 8, 2009, Sotomayor was sworn in as a Supreme Court justice.

In August 2009, Sonia Sotomayor (soh-toh-mye-OR) became a Supreme Court justice. It is a special job. Sotomayor is the 111th person ever to receive that honor. She is the third woman and the first Hispanic justice to serve on that court.

A justice is another name for a judge. There are nine justices on the Supreme Court. They work as a team to make rulings, or decisions. Their rulings become law all across the United States.

Sotomayor (back row, far right) is the first Hispanic justice to serve on the Supreme Court.

Sotomayor had dreamed of being a judge since she was ten years old. She got the idea from a popular television show called *Perry Mason*. Mason was a lawyer working in a courtroom. He was the star of the show, but Sotomayor noticed something else.

Mason would argue his case, but the judge was clearly in charge. Sotomayor wanted to be the judge. But she never imagined that one day she would be a Supreme Court justice.

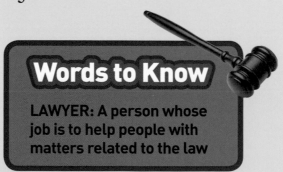

Words to Know

LAWYER: A person whose job is to help people with matters related to the law

In Her Own Words

"I realized that the judge was the most important player in the room."

On an episode of the TV show *Perry Mason*, a judge (middle) listens as Mason (left) questions someone on the stand.

Growing Up in the Bronx

Sotomayor was born in New York City on June 25, 1954. Her parents were from the island of Puerto Rico (PORE-tuh REE-koh). Both of her parents came to the mainland United States in the 1940s. They met in New York City and got married. They settled in a section of the city known as the Bronx.

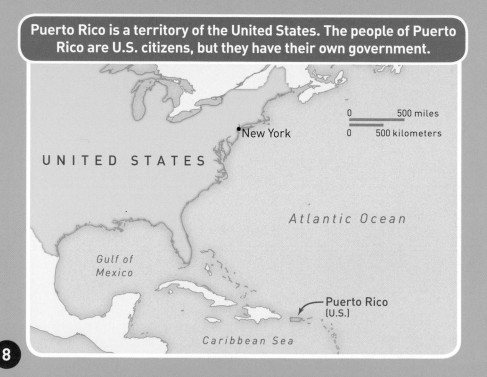

Puerto Rico is a territory of the United States. The people of Puerto Rico are U.S. citizens, but they have their own government.

0   500 miles

0   500 kilometers

New York

UNITED STATES

Atlantic Ocean

Gulf of Mexico

Puerto Rico (U.S.)

Caribbean Sea

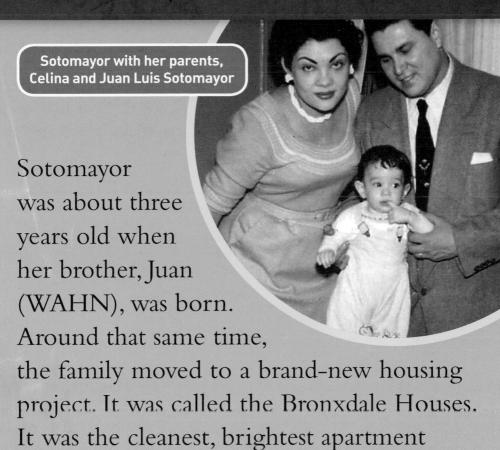

Sotomayor was about three years old when her brother, Juan (WAHN), was born. Around that same time, the family moved to a brand-new housing project. It was called the Bronxdale Houses. It was the cleanest, brightest apartment Sotomayor had ever seen.

Words to Know

HOUSING PROJECT: A group of houses or apartments built with money from the government

One of Sotomayor's grandmothers lived in the area. Aunts, uncles, and cousins also lived nearby. On Saturday nights the family all got together. They played games such as bingo, and there was always lots of food.

Sotomayor with her brother, Juan

Sotomayor enjoyed baseball games at Yankee Stadium.

In the summers, the family enjoyed all-day picnics at Orchard Beach. The Bronx is also home to Yankee Stadium. They liked going to baseball games there. Sotomayor became a lifelong Yankees fan.

That's a FACT! Sotomayor's father did not speak English. At home, the family spoke Spanish.

Being Brave

Sotomayor enjoyed time with her family, but she got tired easily. She was also thirsty much of the time. When she was almost eight years old, she learned why.

Sotomayor had diabetes (dye-uh-BEET-eez). Her body was not able to use sugar the way it should. Doctors told her parents that she needed to use insulin (IN-suh-lun) to treat her diabetes. Insulin is given in the form of a shot. Sotomayor would need shots every day for the rest of her life.

Sometimes Sotomayor's parents argued about who would give her the shots. Sotomayor did not want them to argue about her. She learned to give the shots to herself.

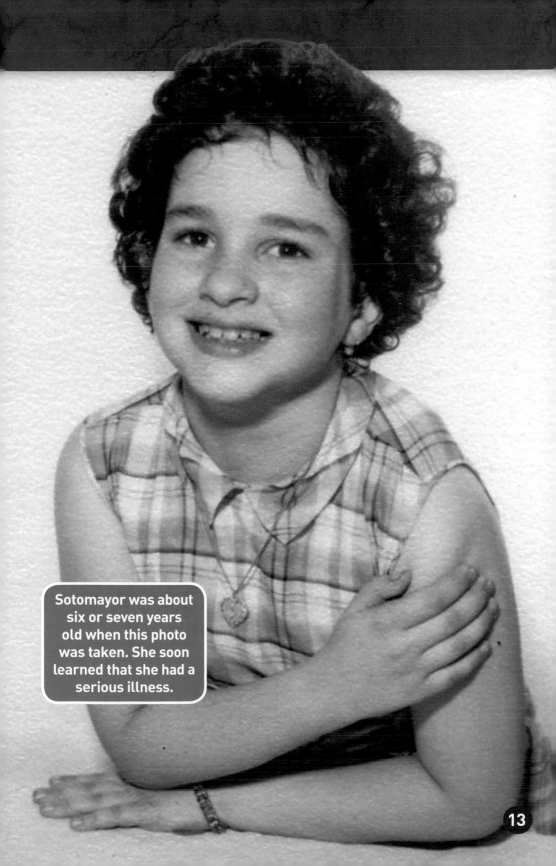

Sotomayor was about six or seven years old when this photo was taken. She soon learned that she had a serious illness.

About a year later, Sotomayor's father died. Her mother was left alone to raise the two children. She worked six days a week to support the family.

Sotomayor's mother taught her children to work hard in school. Sotomayor wanted to be a good student, but she did not know how. So she got help.

That's a FACT! Sotomayor read books to fill the long lonely days after her father died. She especially liked the Nancy Drew mystery series about a girl detective.

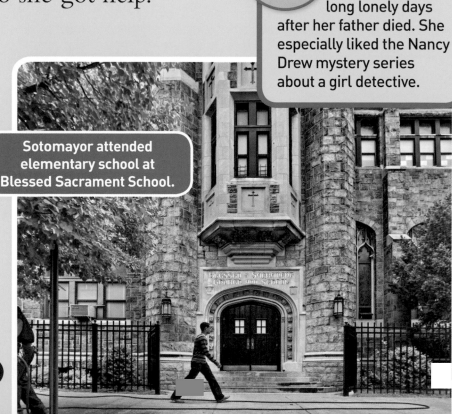

Sotomayor attended elementary school at Blessed Sacrament School.

Sotomayor's eighth-grade graduation photo

She asked one of the smartest girls in her fifth-grade class for some study tips. One tip was to underline important facts as she read. Knowing how to study helped. Sotomayor became one of the top students in her class.

In Her Own Words

"My mom believed that education was the key to everything in the world."

The neighborhood where Sotomayor lived was changing. Gangs were fighting each other. More crimes were happening. When Sotomayor was in high school, the family moved to a safer area in the Bronx.

Sotomayor went to Cardinal Spellman High School. After school, her friends liked to hang out at her apartment. One of those friends was Kevin Noonan. He became Sotomayor's boyfriend.

Sotomayor visits with students at Cardinal Spellman High School.

In 1972, Sotomayor graduated from high school. Her hard work earned her a scholarship to attend Princeton University. It is one of the top schools in the country.

That's a FACT! When Sotomayor was in high school, her mother went back to school to become a nurse. At night, Sotomayor and her mother and brother all studied together at the kitchen table.

Words to Know

SCHOLARSHIP: Money given to a student by a school or group to help pay for the student's education

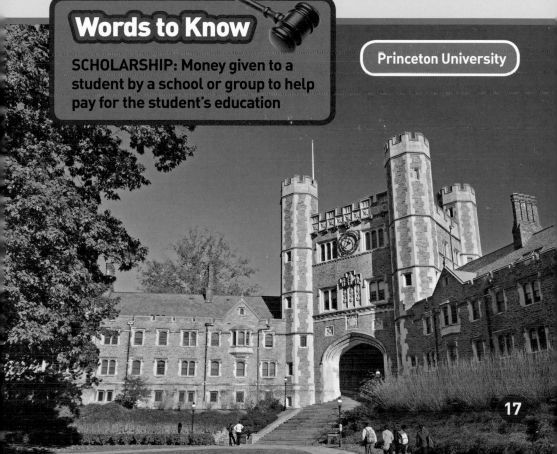

Princeton University

Studying Hard

Many of the students at Princeton were from rich families. Very few of them were women. There were also few Hispanic students. Sotomayor felt like an alien from another planet.

For a while, she never spoke in class. She was too shy to raise her hand. The first paper she wrote was not very good. The teacher marked many places that needed more work. Sotomayor did not give up. Instead, she got help from her teachers and learned to write better. In 1976, she graduated from Princeton with highest honors.

That's a FACT! Sotomayor and other Puerto Rican students worked to bring more Hispanic students and teachers to Princeton.

In Her Own Words

"You have to get up and try again. That's sometimes really hard to do, when you get embarrassed over failure."

a classroom at Princeton

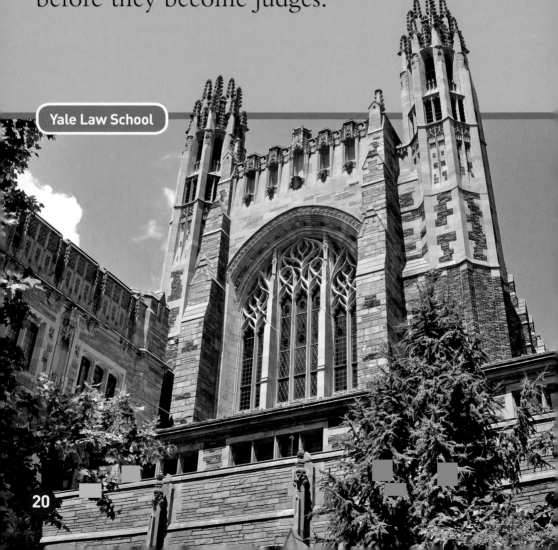

But Sotomayor was not finished with school yet. That fall, she began classes at Yale Law School. To become a judge, she needed to know all about the law. People often work many years as lawyers before they become judges.

Yale Law School

Yale University library

In August,
before school
started, she married
Kevin Noonan. He
had graduated from college too.
He was thinking about going on
to study either law or science.

At Yale, Sotomayor spent a lot of time in
the library studying old court cases. This
helped her learn how lawyers work. She
graduated from Yale Law School in 1979.

Sotomayor's Cool Firsts

Sonia Sotomayor was the first to do a lot of things. Did you know these firsts?

As a senior at Princeton University, Sotomayor became the first Hispanic woman to win the M. Taylor Pyne Honor Prize. It is an award given to outstanding students who are also good leaders.

UNITED STATES

New York

Atlantic Ocean

Gulf of Mexico

She was the first person in her family to be born in the mainland United States.

In 1992, she became the first Hispanic federal judge in the state of New York.

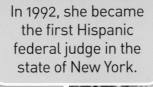

In 1998, she became the first Hispanic woman to serve on the U.S. Court of Appeals for the Second Circuit.

Words to Know

FEDERAL: Having to do with the U.S. government

In 2009, she became the first Hispanic justice on the U.S. Supreme Court.

On New Year's Eve in 2013, she flipped the switch to drop the crystal ball in Times Square in New York City. She was the first Supreme Court justice to take part in that New Year's Eve tradition.

Fighting Crime

Sotomayor's first job as a lawyer was in New York City. She worked in the office of the district attorney (uh-TURN-ee). Police arrest people whom they believe have committed crimes. It was Sotomayor's job to prove in a court of law that those people were guilty.

Her day started at 7:00 a.m. Many days, she did not get home until 10:00 at night. Her husband was busy too. They did not have much time to spend together. Their lives were going in different directions. In 1983, they got divorced.

This is how the skyline looked when Sotomayor was a lawyer in New York City.

Sotomayor worked for five years in the district attorney's office. Then she was ready for a change. In 1984, she joined a small law firm in New York City. Part of her job was to protect companies from people who tried to copy their ideas or products.

Sotomayor still wanted to become a judge. But she could not just get that job on her own. She must be chosen, or nominated. Sotomayor soon got her chance.

Words to Know

NOMINATE: To suggest someone for a job or office

In Her Own Words

"I . . . believe that those of us who have opportunities in this life must give them back to those who have less."

Sotomayor talks with students at her old elementary school, Blessed Sacrament School.

Helping Others

Sotomayor was busy at work, but she found time to help others too. She helped young people learn more about becoming lawyers and judges. She also worked with a group to help get money for families that could not afford housing.

Reaching a Dream

In November 1991, President George H. W. Bush nominated Sotomayor to be a federal judge. It was for a U.S. District Court in the state of New York.

Before Sotomayor could become a judge, the U.S. Senate needed to confirm her. On August 11, 1992, the Senate voted. They agreed to make Sotomayor a federal judge.

She was 38 years old and had achieved her dream of becoming a judge. She also made history. She was the first Hispanic person to become a federal judge in the state.

Words to Know

DISTRICT COURT: A court that handles cases in a particular area of the U.S. This is the first level of federal court.

CONFIRM: To approve someone by voting for that person

As a new federal judge, Sotomayor poses in front of shelves of law books.

Becoming a Federal Judge

Federal judges work for the United States government. The president nominates a person to become a federal judge. The Senate then votes on that person. If the person gets enough votes from the senators, that means he or she is confirmed by the Senate. If that person does not get enough votes, the president must nominate someone else.

Saving Baseball

Sotomayor heard many cases in her court. One of her most famous cases was about a Major League Baseball strike. The baseball players and the team owners could not agree about how the players should be paid. The players went on strike. They would not play any games. Because of the strike, there was no World Series in 1994.

Words to Know

STRIKE: A kind of protest in which a group of people stop work until they are treated better

The case came to Sotomayor's court in March 1995. She listened to the players and to the team owners. Sotomayor agreed with the players. Her ruling ended the 232-day strike. Some people said she saved baseball.

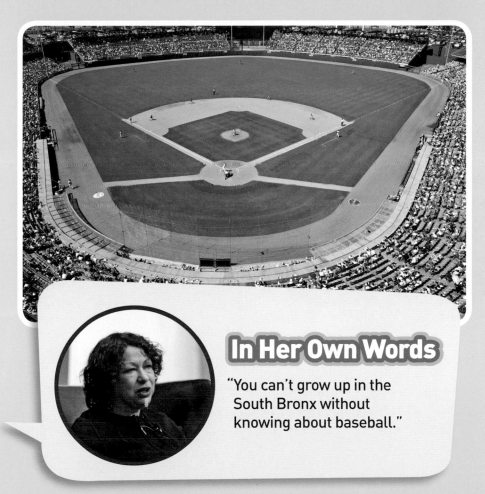

In Her Own Words

"You can't grow up in the South Bronx without knowing about baseball."

6 COOL FACTS
About Sotomayor

As a girl, Sotomayor liked to read comic books. Two of her favorites were about Casper, a friendly ghost, and Richie Rich, a boy who comes from a wealthy family.

1

2

In 2012, Sotomayor traveled to Sesame Street to settle a disagreement between Baby Bear and Goldilocks. Their disagreement was about Baby Bear's broken chair.

As a student at Princeton, Sotomayor challenged herself to learn five new words each day.

3

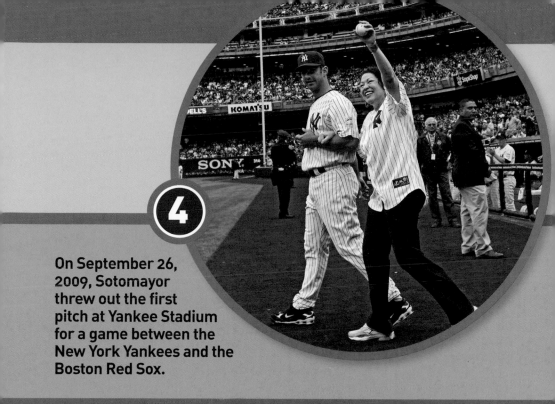

4

On September 26, 2009, Sotomayor threw out the first pitch at Yankee Stadium for a game between the New York Yankees and the Boston Red Sox.

5

On June 4, 2010, the Bronxdale Houses housing project got a new name. It became the Justice Sonia Sotomayor Houses and Community Center.

Sotomayor stays in shape by running on a treadmill in the gym in the Supreme Court building.

6

A Higher Court

Sometimes people believe a court ruling is not fair or right. When that happens, they can appeal. That means they can ask a higher court to hear the case.

The next higher court above the U.S. District Court is the U.S. Court of Appeals. In 1997, President Bill Clinton nominated Sotomayor as a judge for that higher court.

The Federal Courts

THE SUPREME COURT

U.S. COURT OF APPEALS
There are 12 U.S. Courts of Appeals. The Second Circuit, where Sotomayor worked, includes Connecticut, New York, and Vermont.

U.S. DISTRICT COURT
There are 94 district courts in the U.S. Each state has at least one federal district. States that have more people have more districts.

Sotomayor stands in her office soon after being confirmed as a judge in the U.S. Court of Appeals for the Second Circuit.

Once again, she needed to be confirmed by the U.S. Senate. For a while, it looked like that would not happen. Some senators did not want Sotomayor to get the job. It took more than a year for the senators to decide. They finally voted to confirm her on October 2, 1998.

On May 26, 2009, President Barack Obama (right) nominated Sotomayor for the U.S. Supreme Court.

Sotomayor worked as a judge for the U.S. Court of Appeals for 11 years. Then, in 2009, there was an opening on the Supreme Court. President Barack Obama thought about whom he could pick for that court. He had four people in mind. Sotomayor was one of them.

On May 21, Sotomayor met with the president at the White House. He liked the way she answered his questions. He believed she was a good person for the job. On May 26, he nominated her to be a Supreme Court justice.

That's a FACT! The news about Sotomayor's Supreme Court nomination was announced over the loudspeaker at Cardinal Spellman High School.

Sotomayor answers questions from the senators.

Sotomayor still needed to be confirmed by the U.S. Senate. On July 13, she met with a Senate committee, or group. For three days, those senators asked Sotomayor a lot of hard questions. They wanted to be sure she was the right person for such an important job.

In Her Own Words

"I am an ordinary person who has been blessed with extraordinary opportunities and experiences."

On August 6, the whole Senate voted. The vote was 68–31. Sotomayor would be a Supreme Court justice.

Sotomayor was sworn in as a Supreme Court justice by Chief Justice John G. Roberts (far right).

1954
Born in
New York City
on June 25

1962
Learns she
has diabetes

1963
Her father dies

Two days later, Sotomayor was sworn in at the Supreme Court building. Her brother stood next to her. Her mother held the Bible where Sotomayor placed her left hand. Then she raised her right hand and took an oath. She promised to treat all people fairly and to follow the U.S. Constitution in her duties as a Supreme Court justice.

Supreme Court justices serve for life. Sotomayor can serve as long as she wants. The Supreme Court hears about 75 to 80 cases each year. Sotomayor spends many hours studying to get ready for each case. It is a lot of work, but she is used to working hard.

1972
Graduates from
Cardinal Spellman
High School

1976
Graduates from
Princeton University

1979
Graduates from
Yale Law School

Inspiring Others

Sotomayor's success has inspired many people. She grew up in a poor neighborhood. She has lived with a serious illness since she was young. As a Hispanic American, she sometimes felt like she did not belong. Sotomayor overcame all those challenges and reached her dream. She has shown that to be successful, you need to dream big and work hard.

1979
Begins work in the district attorney's office in New York City

1984
Joins a small law firm in New York City

1992
Becomes a federal judge for a U.S. District Court

Sotomayor stands in front of the Supreme Court building.

1995

Rules in a case about a Major League Baseball strike

1998

Becomes a judge for the U.S. Court of Appeals

2009

Becomes an associate justice on the U.S. Supreme Court

QUIZ WHIZ

See how many questions you can get right!
Answers are at the bottom of page 45.

Where were Sotomayor's parents born?

A. Mexico
B. Costa Rica
C. Puerto Rico
D. Cuba

Sotomayor learned she had a serious illness called diabetes when she was about _____ years old.

A. 5
B. 8
C. 12
D. 14

In fifth grade, Sotomayor got some study tips from _____.

A. her teacher
B. another student
C. a tutor
D. her mother

After high school, where did Sotomayor start college?

A. Brown University
B. Stanford University
C. New York University
D. Princeton University

Federal judges are nominated by _____.

A. the U.S. Senate
B. other judges
C. the U.S. president
D. the Supreme Court

Sotomayor reached her dream of becoming a judge when she was _____ years old.

A. 38
B. 42
C. 45
D. 50

What is the highest court of law in the United States?

A. The U.S. District Court
B. The U.S. Court of Appeals
C. The New York City Criminal Court
D. The Supreme Court

Glossary

CONFIRM: To approve someone by voting for that person

FEDERAL: Having to do with the U.S. government

HISPANIC: Coming from or having a family from a country where Spanish is the main language

NOMINATE: To suggest someone for a job or office

SCHOLARSHIP: Money given to a student by a school or group to help pay for the student's education

DISTRICT ATTORNEY: A lawyer who decides whether to start cases against people accused of crimes in a particular area of the U.S.

DISTRICT COURT: A court that handles cases in a particular area of the U.S. This is the first level of federal court.

HOUSING PROJECT: A group of houses or apartments built with money from the government

LAWYER: A person whose job is to help people with matters related to the law

STRIKE: A kind of protest in which a group of people stop work until they are treated better

SUPREME COURT: The highest court of law in the United States

Index

Boldface indicates illustrations.